WHAT READERS ARE SA

Thank you for so poignantly creating a truly meaningful, influential book...absolutely incredible!

Shelby G., IN

Tons of very useful information presented in a non-intimidating way. ...I would highly recommend it to anyone looking to enter the world of being an Entrepreneur.

Susan W., MA

Teaches you skills you can put into practice TODAY. A friend gave me Entrepreneur Unleashed and I was pleasantly surprised. It is written in a conversational tone that is easy to understand, even for someone without a business background. The lessons the author teaches you in this book lay the foundation for your financial freedom. The business plans are realistic - no "get rich quick" schemes, and Greg gives you step-by-step, achievable methods for each type of business plan. Just the marketing plans alone are worth the nominal price of the book.

Even more impressive for me personally was the obvious amount of heart and consideration that went into this book. It is evident that the author has a passion for mentoring others and cares deeply about not only the success of his own family, but also the success of his readers. I am looking forward to future books in the series.

B. Humphreys, F

I was fortunate enough to attend one of Greg's 3 day class His messages were actionable and his ideas help change way I viewed debt and money. In this book Greg's abili coach and inspire in person comes through in a way that al made me feel like Greg was present in the room. I could a hear his voice coming through in the written words.

While many books are entertaining and hard to put down I found this work compelling me to take action. A number of times I had to put it down to take action upon an idea that was presented.

This book complements and adds an extra actionable dimension to many of the ideas presented in Robert Kiyosaki's "Rich Dad" book.

In this book Greg provided me with complementary transformational empowerment thinking. In my opinion "Entrepreneur Unleashed" should be part of any aspiring investor's library.

Thank you Greg for taking the time to place your ideas into this well written book.

J. Licata

A good immersion on the investor mind. Best guide for new entrepreneur. A detail journey in the life of a guy that starting from zero becomes a successful investor.

Pedro

's passion to help others achieve their greatest potential ious in everything he does. If you are ready to make the your life, this is the man you want on your team!

Dorian C., NY

Downing's Entrepreneur Unleashed book after at-
e day course taught by the author. The book
proach for "normal" people to become suc-
eurs. His writing style is clear and direct,
aving a conversation with him. He does not
the-top jargon in an attempt to impress. His
" are great proactive, first person motiva-
that remind you to remain focused, follow

through on your promises (especially to yourself!!), and to understand that "I can't" no longer exists in your vocabulary.

I am looking forward to more from this series!

Avid Aviator

Great for the entire family! I have now read GREGORY DOWNING's new book ENTREPRENEUR UNLEASHED, It is very much needed in today's imploding economy, uncertainty, and need to not only reinforce Wealth insights but also to leave a Legacy in which a Family can participate together. Involving your family in a well researched endeavor not only increases the chances of success it empowers you. Great book, it shows you how to take charge of your life, your future and you're Legacy. It is a bargain even at 4 times the price. Thank you Gregory!

Tim R, FL

A transformation occurred in my thinking and actions that has given me a renewed determination to build a legacy of wealth intelligence for my children and my children's children's children. Thanks to Greg, I woke up this morning with a context for my plan and renewed perspective of my purpose. I believe and am fully convinced that my financial goals are attainable thanks to Greg's skillful and patient instruction. You have opened my eyes, and now I see! Thank you Greg!

Cynthia H-B., MA

Greg is energetic, passionate and knows his stuff!

Erika B, TX

Greg is a fantastic teacher! … straight forward and direct when needed, yet he balances the truth with a genuine caring …he delivered ALL that he promised!

Rita M, FL

I recently graduated with a Master of Management degree and attended a class Greg taught. The education I received was way more valuable than a master's degree in business. I realized that all knowledge is not power, but the right financial knowledge is power. The education I got gives me the power to build wealth safely yet very quickly.

Alla B., TX

…SO incredibly life changing… Greg knows what he is talking about.

David C., CA

His ability to make understandable, real world applications to the subject matter has helped me develop a much greater understanding of real estate and wealth building strategies. In the future I am confident I will look back and attribute much of my success to the coaching and encouragement I have received from Greg.

Andrew F., FL

Gregory Downing taught me and my sister a wealth of information about building and protecting real wealth in a morally-sound, inspiring and actionable way.

Katrina C., NJ

…Life changing…I was touched by the wisdom and guiding principles you have shared including "the win-win solutions for all involved". You have inspired me to take a giant step forward.

Yan L., NY

I am now taking a new perspective on my life and my way of thinking. I can't wait to get started on my new endeavor.

Eric R., CT

Greg is an amazing source of knowledge and insight. He teaches in concise, understandable and captivating ways, and he explained complex subjects, provided relevant examples, and underscored it all with real-life stories.

Collin M., CT

I learned a lot and look forward to starting my personal real estate empire. I am going to use all you taught me to help my current real estate clients as well. Thanks!

Kathy M., MA

THE UNIVERSAL LAWS unleashed

GREGORY DOWNING

LEGACY UNLEASHED SERIES | BOOK THREE

LEGACY unleashed PRESS

Published by Legacy Unleashed Press, Inc.
1179 N. Lion Cub Pt.
Lecanto, Fl 34461

Legacy Unleashed and Mentor Factor are trademarks of Mentor Factor, Inc.

mentor factor

Visit our Web sites:
mentorfactor.com
gregorydowning.com

Editing assistance: Shelby Gullion
Cover Design and Interior Layout: Min Gates Design
Back Cover Photo: Christine Reynolds Photography, Tampa, Florida
(ChristineReynolds.com)

ISBN: 978-1-938047-01-5

This book is printed on acid free paper.

Printed in the United States of America

TABLE OF CONTENTS

INTRODUCTION

What Does It Mean To Be An Entrepreneur?

Is this book for you? Are you an entrepreneur? Whether you are a multimillionaire or an aspiring businessperson, I believe the answer to both questions is yes. We all have the spirit of an entrepreneur within us. It's up to you to decide whether you will awaken and develop this spirit or let its amazing potential lie untapped. The Universal Laws are designed to set you on a path of awareness allowing you to take your life to the next level and decidewhat entrepreneurship means to you.

At the core, The Laws are carefully crafted and cultivated to inspire purposeful change, intentional action, and thoughtful planning.

The word "entrepreneur" is from the French *entreprende* meaning "to undertake" or "to do something." We all undertake *something*, don't we? We get married. We have children. We build a house. We write a book—yet we have no guarantees that the marriage will last, the children will make us proud, the mortgage will get paid off, or the book will find readership (or even get published). And yet we do these things anyway. I believe this makes all of us entrepreneurs. And that's why the Laws in this book naturally apply to all of us and to every life situation, personally, spiritually, and financially.

The Universal Laws Unleashed is more than a text designed exclusively to trigger the excitement of entrepreneurs or stimulate the proactive minds of small- and large-business owners. On a deeper level, this book is written to empower *any* individual to accomplish specific, targetable, even seemingly overwhelming objectives. At the core, The Laws are carefully crafted and cultivated to inspire purposeful change, intentional action, and thoughtful planning. Their strategies and truths apply whether the reader is a student, parent, entrepreneur, current business owner, or simply a goal-oriented, motivated individual seeking to establish a legacy that will last for, and greatly impact, many generations to come. In short, they lay out a proven pathway to personal success—however you, the reader, define it. This means, of course, that the Laws will resonate with the entrepreneur in all of us.

I was not born with great genetic skills that allowed me to become a wealthy entrepreneur. I was not blessed with the brainpower of Einstein or the creativity of Monet. I simply had the desire to change my life, the humility to know I needed to learn how from the experts, and the determination to work toward my goals each and every day.

I tell you this because I do not believe, as so many others apparently do, that you have to be "cut out of a certain mold" to be an entrepreneur. Yes, you may have a few special strengths and traits that will give you an edge—and you certainly should use those strengths to your advantage. But the most critical factor is your ability to make the choice to change your life and to consistently act on that choice. Change happens with a commitment to becoming the master of your destiny and a leader in life.

Ultimately, incorporating the Universal Laws Unleashed into your life and the lives of others within your sphere of influence is a great act of love. It's a way of embracing your passions and giving yourself the tools you need to create a future that is whole, meaningful, and filled with joy. I invite you to join me on this great adventure. By accepting, you are saying *yes* to the life you are meant to live.

Ask and You Shall Receive

MentorFactor.com

You hold in your hands a book that can change your life. If you have read *Entrepreneur Unleashed*, Book Two of the Legacy Unleashed Series, then you know that I teach from a set of proven laws that I often refer to as agreements. I developed *The Universal Laws Unleashed* to propel passionate goal-seekers onto a path of achievement and legacy creation. I also created these Laws to minimize your potential risk and to keep you safe as you pursue your life goals, both business and otherwise.

I have compiled these laws (agreements) into this conven-ient companion book so that *Entrepreneur Unleashed* readers—and others —can have the laws at their fingertips. While I hope that you have read (or will read) *Entrepreneur Unleashed* for its strategies and content, I believe the Laws themselves are so vital to the Legacy Unleashed approach to wealth building that they need to be quickly and easily accessible.

Building Relationships and Wealth to Create a Legacy

Why do you need these Laws *now?* Just take a look around. It's clear there is no better time to take charge of our financial futures, first in our *minds*, then in our *actions*. It's time to reevaluate what it takes to be financially free and act in a deliberate way that will turn things around—in effect, it's time to solve the economic crisis in our country one family at a time. Learning about these Laws (agreements) isn't a "get rich quick scheme," and it won't be a walk in the park—but if you follow the principles I am sharing with you, you can gain control of your future and you will be able to not only live in financial awareness and abundance, but also pass the information on to your loved ones. Together we can set in motion the change that will change the world.

Whether you are already familiar with my work or are being exposed to it for the first time, I am here to serve you and to set you on the pathway to success. These laws will help you develop the leader within and guide you during times of indecision, fear, excitement, and change. In *Entrepreneur Unleashed* I teach you and your children *how* to do just that— in a step-by-step, logical, straightforward and low-risk manner. Before you can implement my plan, however, you must first change the very way you think about the world and your place in it. That's why I feel this book is so important: it zeroes in on the mental and spiritual building blocks that make the rest of the plan possible.

It's Time to Upgrade Your Operating System

Our brains operate much like a computer. From the time we were born until the present day, trillions of bits of information have entered our brain. Based on that information, we have developed internal operating programs and beliefs. Think about it! If you are reading this book and you are 40 years old, you have lived 14,600 days—and that means you are operating on 350,400 hours of old programming. These operating programs are running 24/7 and most of us are as unaware of them as we are of our actual computer's operating system that runs inconspicuously in the background. The system is just "there," and we don't even notice it until the entire system crashes. I seriously doubt that any of you are still using a computer with a Windows 98 operating system—the world has changed too much, technology has changed too much, and our computer needs for speed have changed accordingly. The same is true for the beliefs you have about work, money, debt, credit, and business. NO WONDER SOMETIMES WE GET THE RESULTS WE AIM

> Every second that clicks is gone,
> BUT
> Every second that clicks is the beginning to your new future.
>
> – *Gregory Downing*

FOR AND SOMETIMES THE OPERATING SYSTEM GOES HAYWIRE AND WE END UP IN GRIDLOCK! It is time to update your operating system so you can safely, quickly, and consistently achieve the results you say you want.

Let's face the facts—with the years of information going into our brain, we've been programmed. All of this information has created your current operating systems, which in turn creates your internal conversations about who you are, what you can accomplish, and what you deserve to have. The harsh reality is this: you are exactly where you are in life personally and financially because that is where you have chosen to be, as a result of your present operating programs. From the time we wake up in the morning until the time we go to bed at night, every one of us has these internal conversations. That small still voice inside your head is blasting out your past programming so loudly that it shapes exactly who you are, what actions you take, and therefore, the results you have in the present. The Universal Laws will assist you so that you don't tune out that loud voice of past programing and therefore, allow it to control our future.

I believe you would agree our educational system is not designed to teach people how to build wealth, and that the internal programming we grew up with was also not designed to teach us to become wealthy. Our parents' instilment of internal programming and our educational system both taught us to go to school and get a good job so that someday it would be our turn to have a good retirement. These cultural beliefs and programming might have worked in previous generations but we all know that system is broken for the current generation. Today times have changed, technology has changed, and how to become wealthy has changed. What worked 50 years ago and what worked when you were seven years old must be upgraded to match your needs in today's complex world.

Every agreement/law that I've included in this book, every law that I've written in this book, will be instrumental in helping you upgrade your operating system (programs). Since we all have internal programs and conversations, let's pick the programs we want and ditch the programs that don't work. I'm not talking about what's right and wrong — I'm talking about what works, what doesn't, and what's next.

Universal Law Unleashed : I will remove all unconscious, negative, and scarcity-based programming.

Unleash Your Internal Power Source

Once you remain consciously aware and vigilant about the fact that your subconscious mind tends to dictate your actions, you can put the information to good use. The fact is, your subconscious mind really, really wants to give you whatever you want. You want the very best for yourself and those you love. At the deepest level your subconscious mind also wants the very best for you and the people you love, and will 100% of the time provide you with whatever you ask it for. But in order for that to happen, you have got to start asking it for whatever you want in life instead of what you've been programmed to *believe* you deserve. Let me ask you a question: are you currently a millionaire or a multi-millionaire? If not, would you like to become one? Wanting to become a millionaire and doing it are two different things—and the first step between the two is beginning to reprogram your mind to believe that you deserve it. On the surface, I'm sure every one of you thinks you believe you deserve to become a millionaire, or even a billionaire. The question you have to ask yourself is, "If I'm not already a millionaire, what has held me back up until now?" You may consciously believe you deserve something, but at the deepest level unconsciously you may be holding yourself back due to those old subconscious patterns/cycles, and the resulting internal mental programs you have created since childhood.

Let's talk for a moment about Aladdin's Magic Lamp. Aladdin rubbed his lamp, and out popped a genie. Whatever

Aladdin requested, his wish was granted. Imagine for a moment that your subconscious mind is Aladdin's Magic Lamp. If you tell the genie you want to become a millionaire, guess what it's going to say? "Okay, I will grant you that wish." However, because of your past programs you tell the genie (your subconscious mind,) "I want to be a millionaire, but I guess that just isn't possible because I know I must work 40 hours a week, 60 hours a week, or even 80 hours a week and struggle to survive." In this situation, guess what the magic genie of your mind is going to do? He or she will give you whatever you ask for, EXACTLY the way you asked for it.

Next, consider the quote from the Bible that states, "The love of money is the root of all evil." However, your belief system about what you deserve and what you think about people who have money might cause you to ever so slightly shorten the quote to, "Money is the root of all evil." WOW! It must be very confusing to your genie to constantly get contradictory instructions such as "Money is the root of all evil" and "I want to be a millionaire." The internal genie can't interpret the small distinctions of your past programs. The genie simply follows orders. Consequently, you must get very clear about the direction you want to take in your life and begin asking for things that are in alignment with your new operating system and beliefs. Only then will you begin to take the actions necessary to consistently move toward your real life goals.

In this moment, deciding that this book will empower you to re-program your brain is already changing your future interpretations and internal conversations. Your new "truth" for yourself can now be, "Wow, I'm the one who is helping to turn the economy around. The next three years of my life will be the most profitable ones I have ever lived. It's not the government that will change the economy; it is everyday Americans like me who will have the courage and character to make bold moves and develop the ability to create a legacy for future generations." Hey genie, I am choosing right now, today, to be the master of my destiny. I choose abundance, a legacy for my family, and the desire to become a powerful contributing human being.

Become the Master of Your Future

The Universal Laws (agreements) I have created for you are designed to support you in giving your genie clear, focused directions to follow. Every law *is* an internal agreement and commitment that you are making *with yourself and with your magic genie.* They are "I will" statements that, when mastered and adhered to on a consistent basis, empower you to be the creator of your future rather than someone who is carried along by life's circumstances and past programming. These agreements are about reprogramming your brain to operate from a place of abundance rather than one of fear and scarcity. Your subconscious mind will give you whatever you ask it for. Therefore, the agreements are designed to train your subconscious mind to give you whatever you want in life. ASK AND YOU SHALL RECEIVE.

Universal Law Unleashed : I will always remember that my mind is a wealth-building machine.

I know when you master the Universal Laws you will unleash a power source unlike anything you have ever felt. Yes, I said master. I do not want you to just "learn about" the agreements/laws; I want you to become a master of them. Take a moment to consider the difference between learning about something and actually becoming a master. Constant repetition and application of the information is what allows you to become a master.

When you master a task you no longer have to think about it to accomplish it both safely and quickly. The laws will simply become a part of who you are. Think about it in real-life terms.

You have already mastered certain skills in your life that you may not realize. When you get in your automobile and put the key in the ignition, you don't have to think about where the key goes. You have already mastered that skill. My students always laugh because this example seems like such a simple task, but I remind them how scary it was the first time they got in a car to drive.

At first, beginning the process to become an entrepreneur may seem scary, but as you master the Universal Laws it will become second nature—much the same way as putting the key in the ignition of the car. Once you've infused the Laws into your thoughts, you will integrate them into your actions naturally and without hesitation.

The Universal Law that Gives All the Other Laws Their Power

Universal Law Unleashed : I will always do exactly what I say I will do.

On the surface, many times the laws will seem easy—so I am cautioning you to take a closer look at them, for they are not easy. So at this moment, I am cautioning you to take a closer look at them, for they are not easy. In fact, they are more complex than your conscious mind can imagine. It's when entrepreneurs break these Universal Laws that they begin to work against their own success and happiness. They actually give themselves permission to fail. (This is true not just in business but also in parenting, relationships, health and fitness, and all areas of life.) It is now time to empower ourselves to succeed. So, it becomes easy to see the benefits of keeping these Laws in front of you at all times. They are both the engine that powers your success and the guideposts that keep you on the straight and narrow. People tend to believe that businesses fail because the owner made some big, catastrophic mistake.

That is generally not the way it works. Most businesses fail—or at the very least, struggle—due to the culmination of many smaller errors that have been unconsciously made. Conversely, it is the sum total of all the little things you do right that makes your businesses astoundingly successful. The Universal Laws Unleashed are intended to increase your awareness of what "doing things right" means. (And awareness is the first step in any sort of change.)

Let's take a quick look at the most pivotal of all the Universal Laws: "I will always do exactly what I say I will do." The reason this law is so critical is because it is simple: if you don't adhere to this cornerstone Universal Law, you might as well toss the rest of the Laws out the window. If you don't do what you say you will do, you won't adhere to the other Laws either—since they are literally proclamations on what you intend to do. Most people assume this Law is about keeping your promises to other people. Well, it is—but just as importantly, it is about keeping agreements that you make to yourself. You might read this and think "Yeah, yeah, yeah, I've already heard that one a thousand times." But have you really? Unless it has resonated and reverberated in your heart of hearts and you've practiced it on a daily basis, then you are surely on some unconscious level regularly breaking agreements with yourself.

I encourage you to study this law carefully and spend some time identifying instances when you failed to keep your commitments to yourself. Maybe you promised you'd stop yelling at your child—and yet, the next time he forgot his homework you heard your voice getting harsher and louder. Or you vowed to exercise five days a week, but on day three it was raining so you decided to sleep in instead. Or you committed to set aside 10% of all new money you make in savings, then decided to blow that safety cushion on a new car. You may be shocked to discover how often you let yourself down. But don't berate yourself: awareness is the first step toward change.

How Breaking Even Small Commitments Hurts Us in the Long Run

To express it in simple terms, breaking any kind of commitment—even those that may seem insignificant—hurts us because our subconscious becomes accustomed to our "crying wolf." Then, when we want to make a big change in our lives, our subconscious simply doesn't believe us. I think it's important to understand the mechanism, so I'll share an example. Most of us have been programmed to believe that keeping our word about a $300K promissory note is extremely important. If we don't, our credit will be ruined and we'll look bad. But how do we feel about being two minutes late to a meeting? No big deal, right? Wrong! The subconscious mind makes no distinction between breaking your word over two minutes or breaking it over $300,000 (or a million dollars). Therefore, little by little when you break your word about small things your conscience gets used to it. It seems to be no big deal at the time—but later, when you tell yourself you intend to succeed and create a legacy for yourself and the future of your family, your internal self whispers "Yeah, sure—just like you were going to return the hammer you borrowed from your neighbor." In other words, if that internal voice doesn't believe you then you are doomed to erratic results. Sometimes you pull a magic rabbit out of the hat. Other times, you are up to your neck in alligators. To achieve major life goals, you need the magic rabbit all the time (or at least most of the time). My point? It's very important to start keeping very small promises to yourself on a daily basis. Your internal belief systems will then start to align with what you say you want, and you'll begin seeing the desired results more and more often.

Have you ever wondered why we so willingly and frequently break commitments we have made to ourselves? The number one reason is because there is no accountability associated with these silent promises — no one knows we broke them except for ourselves. Still, as we've just discussed, there is a severe consequence to breaking these commitments: when we don't fulfill them, we are actually giving ourselves permission to fail—and the consequence of this permission is a future unwillingness to keep trying.

Why do we care more about what others think of us than about whether or not we succeed in life? As I've mentioned, much of it has to do with our "programming." We have been programmed and conditioned to keep our word to others at all costs—but few of us grew up with parents who taught us to keep promises to ourselves. And so we're trapped in existing internal conversations that tell us the life we're living now is the life we deserve. I am not suggesting our parents didn't love us and want the best for us Certainly they did. But they, too, were trapped in the same internal conversations they imparted to us. We can only teach our children what we ourselves know. As a result of the programming that has been passed down from generation to generation, most people either a) don't believe they're worthy of building wealth and creating their own future, b) don't know how to do it, or c) both.

> **It is the sum total of all the little things you do right that will make the difference between being average or becoming champions.**
>
> *– Gregory Downing*

How to Use The *Universal Laws Unleashed*

The more you study, absorb, and practice the Laws, the more you will be able to master them - and the more successful you will be in all the ventures you undertake. The more rigorous you are in forming the habits of wealthy people, the more dramatic the results you'll enjoy. Of course, these are not hard and fast rules. These are only suggestions. I *will* promise you this, however: the more you study, absorb, and practice the Laws revealed in the book, the more successful you will be in all the ventures you undertake. The more rigorous you are in forming the habits of wealthy people, the more dramatic the results you'll enjoy. Here are some of the ways you might use this book:

- If you're an entrepreneur following the strategies laid out in *Entrepreneur Unleashed,* refer to *The Universal Laws Unleashed* as needed to keep you on track and moving in the direction to which you've committed. An hour or so spent with the Laws can be especially helpful at those times you find yourself road blocked or paralyzed and need a refresher course.

- If you're not a "traditional" entrepreneur—meaning you don't own a business—you can apply the Laws in this book to any area of life. They will work for anyone in any stage of an array of unique experiences: *The Universal Laws Unleashed* can easily become the laws of becoming a successful student, an inspiring businessman, a creative artist, or a driven humanitarian. They can positively and enduringly shape the actions of any motivated individual who wishes to set goals, actively pursue specific results, and establish enduring legacies in personal, business, or family relationships.

- Use The Universal Laws as a daily affirmation tool. Start your morning by reading a Law first thing. End your day by reading one as well. If you so choose, journal on these Laws (writing can be a powerful way to focus your thoughts and strengthen your intentions). This will spark continued use of the new habits and bring them habitually and readily into the forefront of your mind.

- Share the book with employees and close business associates. You might provide key players with their own copy of this book (and possibly *Entrepreneur Unleashed* as well). You might even consider holding a weekly meeting in which a Universal Law is read and discussed. The more deeply your team is immersed in this world, the more successful your organization will become.

• Share this book with family members, friends and anyone whose lives you wish to enrich and expand. As you know if you're following the strategies in *Entrepreneur Unleashed*, you may find yourself teaching both upward (to your parents) and downward (to your kids) at the same time. The Laws in this book will help everyone you love create a new context from which they can experience life in a new thrilling way. That's the greatest gift and legacy you will ever give.

• You might choose two Laws to focus on and practice each week. One of the Laws could be something you want to improve on. The other could be something that you're already good at. In this way you'll balance tough tasks with more rewarding ones.

The Universal Laws Unleashed

You have brains in your head.
You have feet in your shoes.
You can steer yourself in any direction you choose.
You know what you know.
You are the guy who'll decide where to go.

~Dr. Seuss

MentorFactor.com

THE UNIVERSAL LAWS UNLEASHED

As I mention throughout *Entrepreneur Unleashed*, it took your lifetime, the culmination of every day since you were born, to embed your internal belief systems. You are the sum total of all you currently believe about how the world works, who you are, and your place within it. The Universal Laws will allow you to collapse that time frame and cut to the chase as you pursue your life goals.

For that reason, I have written the following summaries of the laws in first person, and I encourage you to read and reread them to help you speed up the process and move toward financial freedom. By reading them to yourself (and out loud), you will begin the process of speaking to yourself and to others as if the programming has already changed. You will be acting as the creator of your life, and the agreements will not just be mine; they will become yours as well.

Remember, it's never going to be any individual agreement that makes the difference in your life; it's the sum total of all the agreements and their interconnectedness that will have a dramatic impact on every area of your personal, spiritual, and financial life. You will change as a person and grow as a leader and family member when you begin to master these skills. Some of them may seem self-evident - but believe me, I have studied human behavior for many years, and there are very few people who put any of them into practice 100% of the time.

Take complete ownership of each agreement, because when you do, your life and your circumstances will begin to improve. That is when you can begin to take control of your financial future. You may have spent your last dollar to buy this book, or you may already be a millionaire; either way, this book and these agreements can bring prosperity into your life. No matter where you are today in terms of finances, these agreements are designed to take you to the next level. Enjoy the journey knowing there are wonderful days of financial prosperity and family closeness coming your way!

 **Universal Law**

I WILL ALWAYS DO EXACTLY WHAT I SAY I WILL DO

I've heard the message, "I will always do what I say I will do; my word is my bond" throughout my lifetime. I have always thought I understood its meaning, and for the most part, I work to keep the agreements I make with others. However, I am realizing what I really need to examine is, "with whom do I make and then break agreements most often, and why?" Suddenly I realize the one person I break the most agreements with is myself! The truth is, I know when I make agreements with others, and that if I break them, there will be accountability and consequences. On the other hand, when I break an agreement with myself, no one else knows - but my excuse is a justification of my unwillingness to keep my agreement. This law forces me to recognize the fact that when I break agreements with myself, there is accountability and consequences to both my future and my family's future. It is the most important Universal Law of Being an Entrepreneur, because unless I adhere to it, the rest of the agreements become meaningless. When I give my word, I am making an agreement, a promise, and a pact that must be kept. If I don't keep that agreement, I am actually giving myself permission to fail and remain in the same financial situation I am currently in.

It is clear that there are tremendous consequences that result when I break agreements with myself. It is also clear that many commitments I break are broken at an unconscious level, allowing me to just sweep them under the carpet.

Keeping my word is the first step to building my character, and it is the first step to to becoming a leader. Once I have become completely clear about the monumental importance of keeping agreements with myself and with others, I have taken the first step towards building the character and leadership skills that will allow me to create the life of my dreams and a legacy for the future generations.

Universal Law

I WILL HAVE A WRITTEN PLAN FOR EVERY BUSINESS I CREATE

The small business owner begins a business for the purpose of earning a living and creating a feeling of safety and security. In today's tough economic times, this often creates a false sense of security. In contrast, the entrepreneur has an entirely different motivation, and each business is chosen for the purpose of taking the endeavor to its highest level of success. In order to do this, the entrepreneur always formulates, creates, envisions, and writes a business plan that will guide him or her through the stages of creation and growth.

I am committed to evaluating and writing down my plans for the future—and that applies to each business I create. I am committed to building my business streams of income safely, because when I am safe, I will be able to act quickly. Since I have evaluated what my competition, strengths, weaknesses, and expectations are, I know where I am headed and how I intend to get there.

The Universal Laws of Being an Entrepreneur are the backbone of my business plan. I will examine and include the principles I learn in order to ensure my business success. I understand that with these laws in place, my chances of succeeding are extremely high. I live by these laws of entrepreneurship. I know what it will take, I know the pathway to reach my goals, and I trust that my business plan will guide me along the way.

MY NOTES

**Universal Law**

I WILL COURAGEOUSLY MASTER THE ATTRIBUTES OF A LEADER

I understand and accept that the pathway of the entrepreneur is the pathway of a leader. There is joy, financial freedom, and responsibility involved in leadership; if I am truly committed to building wealth and creating a legacy for my family, I must also become deeply committed to growth in character and integrity.

Perception is reality, and no one will follow a leader who does not demonstrate a mastery over themselves. Each agreement I make, I will make with commitment and courage, for I understand that I have chosen a pathway in life that few people have the determination or the character to choose. While none of the agreements I make with myself or with others seem particularly monumental or impossible to achieve when viewed individually, I realize that when viewed as a whole, few people in life are committed enough to master them. However, I also understand that when viewed as a set of standards that make a difference, wealth will come and I will be safe—because each of these agreements contributes to my financial freedom. Today and every day, I choose to lead, grow, and prosper. Life requires courage, and it will take courage to adhere to the principles of leadership. Yet in doing so, I will create a life of financial abundance. As I model The Universal Laws of Being an Entrepreneur, I will build wealth and show others that they can do the same.

**Universal Law**

I WILL CLEARLY DEFINE MY LIFE'S BURNING DESIRE

My life's burning desire is my reason *why*—the reason I am choosing to become an entrepreneur. A big part of my desire revolves around my commitment to build wealth that can stand the test of time. Then, I can pass that knowledge on to my family members and loved ones.

Knowing and understanding my true reason for becoming an entrepreneur accomplishes several things. First and foremost, it allows me to live my dream on my own terms and create my life according to my passion, commitments, and values. In addition, when I have made a commitment to myself and to others based upon that burning desire, my commitment will sustain me and give me the stamina and perseverance to carry on during the times when things do not go as planned, or when the tasks feel overwhelming or even impossible to complete.

 **Universal Law**

I WILL CREATE A LEGACY OF FINANCIAL LITERACY AND ABUNDANCE

I am committed to leaving my mark on the world and being remembered as a person who not only lived and produced heirs, but someone who lived and made a difference. I will create a legacy of financial literacy and abundance that will continue for many generations to come. I know that without my knowledge, courage, and commitment, my family will struggle financially, and for that reason I am determined to reshape the programming of those I love. Then, my loved ones can envision and create a safe and more prosperous future. I also know this will only happen if my programming has changed and I have put into practice these principles of entrepreneurship. My family will then see the possibility of a future that is vastly different than the present. I am a leader, an entrepreneur, and a visionary. I will do whatever it takes to change the world, one family at a time!

**Universal Law**

I WILL TAKE ACTION IN MY LIFE—NOW!

Thinking about building wealth is something people spend their whole lives doing. Yet if I am only thinking about building wealth, I will have nothing but the same old reality. While thoughtfulness and dreaming are important, only action produces results. Each day that passes without action is another day of the status quo. Next week turns into next month, next month turns into next year, and next year turns into never. Life requires action—and action is the catalyst for change. I am totally committed to teaching my loved ones how to create financial abundance - but that means I must take action and do it myself first. They may never see how they should or could behave to create a different reality unless I have modeled it for them.

Every morning I will wake up and ask myself, "What action am I going to take today to move toward my dream of financial independence and self-reliance?" And from that starting point, I will make decisions and act upon those decisions to move one step closer to my dreams. To do otherwise is to look back a month, a year, or even a lifetime later and realize that while I had good intentions, I did not create the results I intended to create.

MY NOTES

 **Universal Law**

I WILL BE MORE AFRAID OF NOT TAKING ACTION THAN I AM OF TAKING ACTION!

The majority of our population has been programmed to be afraid of change and terrified of risk. These two mindsets make us very fearful about trying new things that are outside our comfort zones. Yet when we examine the current state of our economy, we must accept the fact that change is in order.

"If I don't do something different, nothing will change," is my new mantra. Change is needed, and if I don't change I am placing myself at a much higher level of risk than if I take action.

Only action produces change. Thinking about change, planning to do it, and talking about it is only my way of pretending to take action. The reality is that nothing changes until I change. Someday is not a day of the week.

From this moment on, I will look at my life and my finances in a rational and realistic manner—and take actions for the purpose of creating wealth. I will reprogram my old beliefs about change, and the changes I make today will bring me to new heights of achievement.

 **Universal Law**

I WILL REMAIN PASSIONATE ABOUT THE VISION I SEE FOR MY LIFE

The key word for me in this agreement is "remain." It's easy to get excited about something and say we are passionate; it's even easy to be passionate for a period of time. However, to remain passionate we must have the clarity and deep commitment that few people ever achieve. The vision I see for my life comes from a passion that is bigger than me; it comes from commitment that is about more than money.

When I become very clear about my vision and my passion, the mechanism to achieve the vision I have for my life becomes very clear as well. My vision for my life and for my family is the driving force behind my burning desire, and that vision keeps me going during times of tribulation, distraction, and crisis. When I encounter obstacles, I can always return to my vision for my family and for others—and that reignites my passionate fire that is bigger than any circumstance or obstacle I encounter.

As I reach toward my goal, my vision is greater than simply building wealth and achieving financial freedom: my vision is about others as well as myself. It is about creating a legacy of ffinancial independence that remains long after I have left this world, continuing to produce wealth for my loved ones as well as as passing that knowledge on to their children.

I am passionate about my life and my vision for the mark I will leave upon this world. Nothing will stop me, nothing will hold me back, and nothing will discourage me. My reason *"why"* is greater than any obstacle I might face. My vision is attainable, and by keeping my eye on the goal and moving toward my dreams, I will be modeling courage, commitment, and passion for others—inspiring them to do the same.

 **Universal Law**

I WILL ALWAYS REMEMBER THAT MY ACTIONS ARE NOT BASED UPON LIFE'S CIRCUMSTANCES

Circumstances are guaranteed to kick in as soon as I make a choice to change both my present and future financial situation. My commitment, then, must be bigger than the circumstances I am confronted with. Although at this moment I may be completely committed to taking action, as life's circumstances and my internal programs pop up, they can cause me to fail. I understand that I cannot succeed unless I am willing to start—to take steps that move me toward my dreams and goals—and then keep going even if I have a mountain to climb. Circumstances are nothing more than situations that need to be handled. The circumstances of life are a challenge for everyone. Those who develop the ability to confront challenges and work through them are the people who reach their goals. Some people use circumstances as an excuse to remain the same—and as result, they accept the status quo.

I accept that I will have circumstances and challenges to overcome as I go through the process of becoming an entrepreneur. My circumstances, however, will not control my life!

 **Universal Law**

I WILL REMOVE ALL UNCONSCIOUS, NEGATIVE AND SCARCITY-BASED PROGRAMMING

It is time for me to consciously replace old negative mindsets with ideas and actions that will create a life of abundance and a legacy for future generations. This will sustain me as I begin thinking and acting in ways that will meet my needs. What I believed about the world when I was seven years old does not necessarily work for me today, and I must upgrade my belief systems so that they are consistent with my needs in today's complex world. The programs I grew up with were not designed to teach me how to attain wealth.

Today and every day, I will evaluate and reconsider what works for me as I move toward living a life of wealth and abundance. That means I understand what risk is, how to handle it, and how to balance risk versus reward. In turn, I will become a calculated risk taker. When I discover an opportunity to build wealth, I will look closely at my emotions, my willingness to take action, and my desire to move forward. If I realize I am emotionally resistant due to fear or feelings of uncertainty, I will calculate the risk versus reward and allowing me to move forward. Through this process of evaluation, I will begin to re-invent my beliefs about the fear of investing, the availability of money, and the lack-mentality that has been programmed into my being since the day I was born.

It is time for me to remove all unconscious, negative, and scarcity-based programming and consciously replace it with ideas and actions that will create a life of abundance and a legacy for future generations.

**Universal Law**

I WILL ALWAYS GIVE MY 100%, 100% OF THE TIME!

The essence of this agreement revolves around my knowledge that life has, at times, been an emotional roller coaster ride. Sometimes I have felt as if I was giving life 110%, while on other days, I have felt as if I could only give 90%. From this moment on I will remember that it is possible to give my all every day of my life. I only have 100% and I can never give more than that. Sometimes this emotional roller coaster ride is a result of my getting excited about the next big thing and going full-steam ahead, but not having a formulated plan with a systems, a team, knowledge, or a mentor to help me execute the plan.

Life does not have to be chaotic. If I begin each day with a reaffirmation of my vision and desire for the future, I will feel more encouraged and have more energy to keep the commitments I have made to myself. Each morning I will remind myself that I am the foundation of my wealth and the creator of my future. I will soon become more confident, and that confidence will fuel my ability to give my 100%, 100% of the time.

 **Universal Law**

I WILL REMAIN AWARE THAT I AM 100% RESPONSIBLE, 100% OF THE TIME, FOR THE RESULTS IN MY LIFE

I know, at least on an intellectual level, that no one is going to build wealth for me; if I truly want to become financially free, I have to create my life and set things up to make my dream come true.

The truth is that I am 100% responsible 100% of the time for the results in my life. I commit to becoming consciously aware that I am the only one who can create a life of financial abundance and generational legacy.

Every morning from today forward, I will make a commitment to do one small thing that moves me one step closer to financial independence and freedom. It might be a fresh approach to an old problem, it may involve my stepping out of my comfort zone, but from today onward, I will devote a portion of every single day to my future and to my goals.

Life has a way of kicking in—there are bills to pay, problems to solve, and circumstances that need attention. I will not allow these things to stop me, because today, and every day, I will make the time to move toward the life of my dreams!

Universal Law

I WILL REMAIN CONSCIOUS THAT MY FAITH EQUALS MY FOLLOW-THROUGH

There are probably hundreds of times I have made a decision and then doubted it, changed my mind, or blamed someone else for my lack of commitment. The underlying reason people tend to revert back to what they are used to doing is a lack of trust in themselves. That old tape begins running every time we step out of our comfort zone. Fear causes me to make excuses and go back to "where it's safe."

One of the ways we justify this behavior is by questioning the decisions we have made. Sometimes I think, "If I do this, and it doesn't work, it will ruin me." My willingness to change these internal mental programs will enable me to realize that my commitment to the project is what carries it through.

All that stands between me and wealth is the knowledge and the commitment to build it. Tasks are only hard when I don't know how to perform them. The laws of becoming an entrepreneur will allow me to create financial abundance without working myself to death. Entrepreneurship is not reserved for the elite few. Entrepreneurship is a learned skill that I am mastering.

 **Universal Law**

I WILL ALWAYS REMEMBER THAT MY MIND IS A WEALTH-BUILDING MACHINE

Building wealth starts with an idea; it begins in the mind. Understanding this, I realize I have to feed my mind in order to make my wealth grow. I will devote both time and energy to growing in financial literacy and character. I will increase my knowledge in all areas of entrepreneurship and leadership.

As I constantly feed my mind with financial intelligence, the knowledge allows me to change my past beliefs and programs so I can make better decisions about my financial future. I will invest in myself, because when I do, my wealth-building process will become second nature. As a result, I will have the ability to teach these lessons to others—creating a legacy of wealth for many generations to come. The world is changing at an alarming rate. With technology, what is current and relevant today is old news tomorrow. This means that throughout my life as an entrepreneur I must be able to take in new information and use it to build wealth and legacy.

**Universal Law**

I WILL INVEST IN A FINANCIAL EDUCATION PROGRAM TO MASTER THE SKILLS OF BEING AN ENTREPRENEUR

It is my goal and my commitment to learn the skills of entrepreneurship, and I understand that building wealth is not going to happen with a get - rich-quick scheme. It is going to take work, dedication, and commitment, as well as an increased level of knowledge. I have been programmed from childhood to go to school, be a good student, and prepare myself for getting a good job that will provide me with a good standard of living and a decent retirement. However, today's educational system doesn't work in the new normal, and I must learn the skills of entrepreneurship if I want to generate multiple streams of income.

The current educational system is not designed to prepare us to become financially self-reliant. It is instead built around preparing its graduates to give the best years of their lives to employers so they can retire on 40% of what they made when they were working. Added to that, in our new world of corporate downsizing and cutbacks, there are not nearly enough good jobs out there for the employees to get.

I am committed to obtaining a new type of education that focuses on the skills of entrepreneurship. Then, and only then, will I be prepared to handle what comes my way—both in terms of opportunity and setbacks—without feeling overwhelmed or lost in the process.

 **Universal Law**

I WILL LIVE MY LIFE WITH THE BELIEF, "IF I CAN'T, I MUST! IF I CAN, I WILL! FAILURE IS NOT AN OPTION!"

Every entrepreneur hits roadblocks and obstacles along the pathway to financial freedom. Growth means change, and the process of change includes new tasks that might seem overwhelming. Knowing this, I must live by the law, "If I can't, I must! If I can, I will! Failure is not an option!" Because if I don't, I will give up when challenges come my way; I will be stopped by my old programming and belief systems about what is possible. Getting out of my comfort zone creates the fear of making changes, fear of risk, and my old programming pops up telling me to hold on to what I've worked so hard to achieve.

From today forward, I will remove the phrase "I can't," and reprogram my brain to tell myself "I must." This doesn't mean that I will succeed at everything I do in life, but it does mean I have attempted to succeed and I have made progress toward my goals. I will be on the alert for times when I think, "I can't do it," because I now realize that every single time I overcome an obstacle that seemed insurmountable, I have changed as a person and grown as a leader. The phrase "I must" will become a gigantic clue that I am ready for my next breakthrough!

**Universal Law**

I WILL LIVE MY LIFE WITH THE BELIEF THAT IF SOMEONE ELSE CAN DO IT, I CAN DO IT!

From today forward, whenever I tell myself "I can't do it," I will follow that statement up with the question, "Can others?"? I know my intelligence level is normal, and anything that needs to be done is simply a matter of having the knowledge, skills, and perseverance to get it done. When I encounter challenges in building my streams of income and come up against a brick wall, I am determined to find out what I don't know, learn it, and then continue to move toward my goals. I realize that the difference between the wealthy and the middle class is knowledge and action.

The world is filled with people who look with longing at those who have conquered the skills of entrepreneurship. I realize those people are just people who had a high level of knowledge, determination, and commitment to their goals. I have that same determination and commitment-and I will do whatever it takes to see my dreams come true. I will build wealth and I will create a legacy for future generations.

**Universal Law**

I WILL REMAIN COACHABLE

The greatest athletes in the world have coaches, and the President of the United States has advisors. Why would I be different? Someone knows what I don't know and someone has already done what I want to do. I am committed to having a mentor who will help me put my new knowledge into action for the purpose of minimizing the mistakes I might otherwise make as I begin my life as an entrepreneur.

My mentor will be there to guide me, to advise me, and will assist me; he or she will not be there to tell me what I want to hear, but to tell me what I need to hear. And in the process, I will remain coachable and open to learning new ways of approaching business problems.

I am committed to becoming a professional entrepreneur with the tools and skills to guarantee my success. Just as the greatest achievers in the world have assistance in accomplishing what others only dream of, I intend to have that same level of assistance so I can realize my vision and create a legacy that will serve my family for generations to come.

I WILL BECOME CLEAR ABOUT THE DISTINCTION BETWEEN LEARNING AND MASTERY

Learning to ride a bike and mastering that same skill are two entirely different concepts—and the difference is the ability to do the task on autopilot. When I have repeatedly accomplished a task so many times that it becomes automatic, it frees my mind up to plan the next step in my wealth-building process. Before I have mastered a skill, it takes all my concentration to do it well. On the other hand, when I have mastered a skill, I have become unconsciously competent in this area—I don't have to think about it—I just do it.

My first business will be the most challenging to create because I will be simultaneously learning many new skills. The second one will be easier because I will have the experience that I gained during the first process. Even though the business endeavors may be unrelated, there will be processes and systems that are similar, regardless of the type business I am working on.

This means that with every new business venture, I will use the knowledge and expertise I have gained, making it easier to master the skills of creating duplicable systems and processes.

MY NOTES

 **Universal Law**

I WILL STOP DOING MINIMUM-WAGE ACTIVITIES

I have been programmed my entire life to believe that if I want the job done right, I have to do it myself. I heard it from my parents, my peers, and my teachers. That old program is deeply ingrained in my psyche, and I must replace it with a new one that sounds like this: "I will learn to work smart, so I don't have to work so hard." One of our culture's most highly touted virtues is hard work—good old 'blood, sweat, and tears'. However, the work of an entrepreneur is the work of the mind. It is the thinking, the planning, the creating, and the oversight of my burning desire and my vision. It is time to redefine my role as a worker.

A business must have strong leadership and vision—without those attributes, even the best of businesses will fail. Knowing this, I must leave tasks that can be accomplished by others to people who have the knowledge and skills to do them—and spend my time as the creator of my businesses and my future. It is my job to watch the bottom line, create the next big idea for growth, and open the next stream of income. I commit to creation—and I will keep that commitment and master it. In doing so, my businesses will prosper and my wealth will grow exponentially.

 **Universal Law**

I WILL TAKE FOUR MONTHS OF VACATION EVERY YEAR

My past programming has conditioned me to believe that I should expect to have two weeks of vacation every year. During good economic times, I spend at least part of that time actually going somewhere, exploring my world, and expanding my vision of what's out there. Given today's tough economic conditions, many of those who are able to take vacations don't spend their time enjoying their family, exploring, or expanding their visions—they spend their time in emotional shutdown worrying about how much money they are spending.

It's time for me to change my programming and begin to live life on my own terms. As an entrepreneur, there is nothing illogical about my working three weeks and taking the fourth off to think, meditate, explore, and expand my business and financial vision. There is nothing illogical about blocking off one month a year to plan and dream for the future. Beginning right now, today, I will work toward the goal of setting aside time to plan and dream.

Right now, this agreement seems like one of those things that "I can't" do. I'm going to stop kidding myself about what I can and can't do, because as I learn to create multiple streams of income, I can begin to live life on my own terms. The money will be there, and I will use my time to learn, enjoy, and create the life I have previously only dreamed of.

I know in my heart that entrepreneurs must set aside time to develop the leadership capabilities that most small business owners do not have. Today and every day, I will work with a goal in mind—to have the time and the resources to enjoy my life doing the things that are meaningful to me.

 **Universal Law**

I WILL ALWAYS REMEMBER THAT TIME IS MORE VALUABLE THAN MONEY

The true entrepreneur understands that time is the most valuable resource. Once it is gone, it can never be regained. For that reason, I will always remember that time is more valuable than money - especially because I can make more money, but I cannot make more time. Knowing this, I treat time as a precious commodity, and I use it wisely and efficiently. This concept is in sharp contrast to my childhood programming. I was taught that time is money and that the way to get ahead in life was to trade my time for money. Yes, I will work hard, but I will also learn to work efficiently. In addition, I will use the time I have available to work toward the creation of my future instead of working to do tasks that I could have others do.

As an entrepreneur, I can and will devote my time to creating wealth, planning and building business systems, and leading my team. Then and only then will I be able to use this precious resource to the best of my ability. Every moment counts, and I will treat time as a stepping stone to moving toward my dreams.

 **Universal Law**

I WILL, WITHIN 12 MONTHS, HAVE THE ABILITY TO LEAVE MY CURRENT JOB WITH NO LOSS OF INCOME

Up until now, I have spent my life working for dollars to compensate for my time. My past programming prepared me to accept this exchange and to believe there is a limited amount of money I can make in any given period of time. That is the problem with living in a world of earned income.

My internal mental programming was focused around working for someone else and making my money based upon the skill I was trained for. Today, I will begin to focus on finding opportunities and replacing my income with a business that will increase my revenue. I realize now that one of the things that has held me back was the very job I'm tied to. Beginning today, I will seek to find businesses that allow me to trade my knowledge for money. Once I have replaced my job with an income stream that takes much less time, I can do it again and again.

Today is the day that I begin choosing to create multiple streams of income. Then and only then will I be empowered to change my perceptions about how hard it is to earn money and how much time it takes to accomplish my financial goals.

 **Universal Law**

I WILL, WITHIN TWO YEARS, HAVE $200,000 IN LIQUID RESERVES

The problem with tragedy is we don't typically receive a 90-day notice before it comes. Then when it arrives, we are not prepared to deal with it on an emotional or financial level. However, there are things I can to do to protect myself financially. I am committed to being prepared for the unexpected. Americans spend most of their lives in an emotional state of financial uncertainty. They have little or no control over their income level or rising prices and have limited savings to fall back on. When an emergency arises, they are not ready to handle the situation. As an entrepreneur, I have more power to control my cash and a greater ability to create it.

Beginning today, I will set aside a minimum of 10% of all new money I create. I am fully committed to having at least $200,000 in a reserve account within the next two years. Now that I understand the importance of reserve accounts, I also understand that failure is not an option.

My long-term and most important goal for the future is a life of financial freedom and providing a legacy. My reserve account is my safety net; it will see me through times of unexpected events that are beyond my control. I have a plan, I will take steps to realize that plan, and the money will follow. I will live by this agreement and do whatever it takes to make it happen!

 **Universal Law**

I WILL MASTER A MINIMUM OF EIGHT STREAMS OF INCOME

Most Americans have one job that brings them a paycheck. Indeed, this is an accepted way of life throughout the United States. However, I no longer buy into that program; instead, I am committed to building wealth through multiple streams of income.

Within the next two years, I will be generating wealth from a minimum of eight streams of income. These revenue sources will include earned, passive, and portfolio income on a continual basis, and if one of them decreases due to the economy or any other reason, I will have at least seven others that continue to meet my financial needs.

No longer will I lie awake at night worrying or wondering where the next paycheck is coming from. I will have done what I needed to do to build my wealth. During the next 24 months, I will keep my eye on the goal. The system will be in place, beginning with quick turn income from real estate transactions. I will get the first stream of income up and running, and then move on to the next one until the money is coming to me in bucket loads. I will always remember, "If someone else can do it, so can I," and I will do whatever it takes to achieve my goal of financial freedom.

 **Universal Law**

I WILL USE MY EXISTING RESOURCES TO BUILD MY BUSINESSES

My past internal mental programming has cautioned me to play it safe and avoid risk. However, I now have new programming that encourages me to think differently about using my existing resources to build my businesses. I am no longer terrified of risk because I have mastered the skills of becoming a calculated risk taker. I have three resources that will help me build my wealth: time, credit, and money.

Time is my most valuable resource because once used, it's gone forever. Rather than living a life of reaction to current circumstances, I will schedule my time and my tasks for the purpose of creation and planning. If I can hire someone else to do jobs I can teach them, I will do so. That frees up my time to continue the process of creating multiple streams of income.

Credit is another one of my resources that I will respect, appreciate, and build. Regardless of where my credit score is today, I will develop a plan allowing me to monitor and increase my score. I will seek the advice of professionals as I begin this process. Credit is something to be used, not hoarded; the more I use my credit to assist me in building wealth, the higher my score becomes.

The final resource I will learn to utilize is money. Money is meant to be moved and leveraged. I will become a master at leveraging my buying ability by using the cash I have to get more. I will also use my money to gain the expertise and knowledge I need to increase my financial literacy and obtain the tools of a professional in each of my streams of income. All three of these resources will propel me to the next level of wealth. I will become a master at taking advantage of my resources in order to collapse time frames and build my wealth safely and quickly.

**Universal Law**

I WILL MAINTAIN A CREDIT SCORE OF 760 OR HIGHER

The way money is controlled when it comes to lending is through credit score ratings. If lenders want to release money into the marketplace, they lower the scores for qualifying. If they want to decrease the flow of cash, they raise qualifying guidelines and scores. In 2011, the scoring for "A" credit was raised to 730. Therefore, I choose to have A+ credit with credit scores that are 760 or higher.

When I do this, it will allow me to be able to borrow more money when I need it. When I have A+ credit, I will also pay lower interest rates, and the cost of doing business will be lessened as I build my streams of income. I will become a master of understanding, evaluating, and controlling my credit scores and credit availability.

I will master the financial tools of literacy, and I will understand wealth accumulation techniques. Credit scores and credit usage are a part of that process. I understand there is plenty of money out there. I will become a master at finding ways to move it from others to me.

 **Universal Law**

I WILL NO LONGER VIEW DEBT AS NEGATIVE, BECAUSE I WILL USE CREDIT TO INVEST SO I CAN GET OUT OF DESTRUCTIVE DEBT FOR THE REST OF MY LIFE

My past internal mental programming has taught me to fear debt and to avoid it. I understand it is not debt that is bad, but the way the average American uses it that is destructive. From today forward, I will use debt to invest and build my wealth. I will reprogram my mind to understand how to invest, using debt and credit to build wealth. Debt allows me to exercise the power of leverage - and it can make me rich. In order to begin the process of reprogramming my mind, I will use the following set of principles and standards for making decisions about debt:

- Will this purchase move me closer to wealth?

- Will it be tax deductible?

- Will it give me a good Return on Investment (ROI)?

- Am I purchasing assets that will appreciate?

- Will it make me more money than the cost of borrowing?

- Will it create cash flow?

When I can answer "Yes" to all or most of these questions, I will view that debt as good debt instead of viewing it as negative. As an entrepreneur, I understand the way the system works, and I will work the system to my advantage.

 **Universal Law**

I WILL NO LONGER LISTEN TO PEOPLE WHO ARE NOT WHERE I WANT TO BE FINANCIALLY

The people with the least amount of money tend to have the most advice when it comes to building wealth. I will instead listen to my mentor and coaches and learn from them. I no longer take advice from people who live in a world of earned income, with only one stream of cash flow, who believe the best way to get through life is to go to work day after day and live on a tight budget. Maybe that works for them, but that is not the way to build a life of financial abundance nor is it the way to create a legacy of financial literacy for my family.

Beginning now, I will seek advice from those who are where I want to be financially. I respect others' opinions, but that does not mean I accept them. I realize and understand that I am on a different financial path than most people. I have courage, confidence, and knowledge to guide me.

 **Universal Law**

I WILL, WITHIN 12 MONTHS, BE COMPLETELY FREE OF DESTRUCTIVE CONSUMER DEBT

While I have redefined my beliefs about investment debt, I have also become crystal clear about the destructive nature of consumer debt and the purchase of items that do not make me money and do not move me closer to wealth. I understand that consumer debt is running rampant in our society. It keeps people tied to their jobs and broke.

I'm committed to changing my conversation about how and why I work. Destructive debt is holding our country in the vicious cycle of work, pay, work, pay, work, pay. As I become free of destructive debt, I will have the ability to change past internal mental programs into new ones. This change will allow me to set my mind free and change the conversation from "I owe, I owe, it's off to work I go" to, "Free at last, free at last!"

Now that my mind is free I will give my 100%, 100% of the time. My new focus is on creating multiple streams of income and becoming free of consumer debt. I am living by the principles of wealth accumulation and financial freedom.

 **Universal Law**

I WILL ALWAYS CREATE
WIN/WIN SOLUTIONS

As I build wealth, I will always work toward creating win/win solutions. First and foremost, I do this because it's the right thing to do. I understand and embrace the belief that when I choose to do the right thing, blessings come back to me tenfold. But it is more than that; I live by the commandment, "Do unto others as you would have them do unto you." I can build wealth without becoming greedy.

When I am considering a business venture, I always look for the win/win solution. If it is a pre-foreclosure deal, I am helping the family in financial straits to move past their current circumstances and situation. I realize that the people I help are looking for someone who will solve their problem and help them move forward. That person is me.

I always remember: on each and every business encounter, if the person I am doing business with doesn't feel honored, appreciative, and thankful after working with me, then I have not kept my commitment. It isn't about working for free and it isn't about forfeiting profitability; it is about acting in a way that finds solutions that benefits everyone involved.

 **Universal Law**

I WILL FULFILL THE UNMET NEEDS
OF OTHERS

I am consciously and consistently aware that a business succeeds or fails based upon its ability to fulfill its clients' needs. In today's highly competitive world, there are businesses on every corner - and each of those businesses is my competitor. It is only when I have my eye on what I can do that others are not willing to do that I can compete and win customers over to my corner.

Unmet needs are not always readily apparent or visible. The questions I have to ask myself as I begin any business are, "What problems are keeping my potential customers awake at night? What do they want that they are not getting?" When I can identify what my clients need, the next thing I must do is create a unique and different approach to the delivery of that product or service. When I can supply a delivery mechanism that simplifies or enhances their lives, I have fulfilled their needs and begun the process of solving their problem.

**Universal Law**

I WILL ALWAYS BE ON TIME

I am deeply committed to doing exactly what I say I will do, and that commitment begins with keeping my time commitments. I will not be disrespectful to others simply because I have not managed my time. This is a major principle of leadership that often goes unnoticed. I am aware that the first five minutes of a meeting set the mood. I will be punctual, knowing it is unacceptable to keep others waiting on me. I am not more important, and my time is not more valuable than anyone else's. I also realize if I am late to an appointment, the relationship I was meant to create has just had to survive a broken agreement. That diminishes trust and disrupts the relationship.

Today and every day, I will remember that a big part of life and leadership revolves around showing up on time. So, I will always show up on time. I am fully conscious of how important this is to my success, I accept it, and I live by this agreement.

MY NOTES

Universal Law

I WILL LEARN TO BUILD MY WEALTH SAFELY AND QUICKLY

There is an art to building businesses—it is an act of creation to become an entrepreneur, and I am committed to the art of building wealth both safely and quickly. These are two keys of entrepreneurship that most small business owners miss. They have been programmed to look at risk and run the other way. They see the risk and forget about balancing the risk with the potential reward.

Many people mistakenly believe that being an entrepreneur is all about being a risk taker. I am not a big risk taker. I have learned instead to be a calculated risk taker who balances risk with potential reward. Whenever I am contemplating a new business endeavor, I will always ask myself, "Do I have the right mentors, power team, knowledge, and expertise to make this business work?" That decreases my risk level and increases my potential for reward. The next question I ask is, "What are the best- and worst-case scenarios for this business?" In other words, what will my return on investment (ROI) be? And then, finally, I ask, "If the worst-case scenario transpires, how would I handle it?"

If I can handle the worst-case scenario and I like the best-case scenario, I have calculated the risk on what it takes to be safe and I have freed my mind from fear. This allows me to give my 100% 100% of the time as I build my wealth quickly.

MY NOTES

 **Universal Law**

I WILL BECOME A MASTER AT CREATING SYSTEMS AND PROCESSES

Becoming a master at creating systems and processes means I will learn and then master the steps in a business's system, and then build a team to help execute those steps. When I have the knowledge, systems, and processes in place that create an efficiently run business, my life becomes simpler. It isn't easy to master the planning steps of building a business, but running a business becomes very simple when I have these systems in place. When I create systems that are duplicable, I have created the process with detailed procedures. I have, in fact, ensured that the process can be duplicated over and overwithout my running the day-to-day operations.

When these business systems are written down, clearly defined, and explained to my team, the jobs get done and the business runs smoothly. Now I am free!

Universal Law

I WILL MASTER THE ART OF BUILDING WEALTH THROUGH ALL THREE TYPES OF INCOME

Out of necessity, employees and specialists live in a world of earned income—they exchange hours of their lives for dollars. I realize there is a purpose for each income type. As an entrepreneur, I understand it is imperative to utilize all three types of income: earned, passive residual, and portfolio.

I will use earned-income businesses that offer big payoffs in short periods of time. These investments will create quick cash so I can then invest in passive or portfolio investments. The most common form of earned income comes from any investment that results in a quick turnaround for a profit.

Earned-income deals produce capital for passive residual purchases, such as buy and hold properties that produce recurring income. This money comes to me day after day, week after week, and month after month. One of the most common forms of passive residual income involves buildings that are rented out and produce monthly positive cash flow.

Portfolio income opportunities typically require hefty cash investments. One of these would be investments in tax liens that earn as much as 25% ROI. This allows me to invest with little time involved and still see strong results.

By balancing and choosing from the three types of income income (Earned Income, Passive Residual Income, and Portfolio Income), I can build wealth efficiently and with much less stress.

Universal Law

I WILL BUY AND SELL TO CREATE CASH SO I CAN BUY AND HOLD TO CREATE LONG-TERM WEALTH

I am committed to achieving financial freedom, and I know that I must create passive residual income that requires little involvement on my part. I will use earned income (quick turns) for the purpose of generating down payments, closing costs, and maintenance and repair money. Professional entrepreneurs have a plan in place that allows them to generate large quantities of cash in short periods of time, and they use that money to fund other types of deals that will give them freedom.

I am committed, and I will do whatever it takes to both replace my current job's income and build a real estate portfolio that includes passive income-producing properties. I will build wealth that stands the test of time and gives me the freedom to live the life of my dreams!

 **Universal Law**

I WILL BUILD THE RIGHT RELATIONSHIPS WITH THE RIGHT POWER TEAM MEMBERS

I am not building small businesses that are operated and run exclusively by me. I am instead in the business of entrepreneurship, and I am always creating new streams of income—that is my primary responsibility. Knowing and understanding the importance of this, every business I create will have duplicable systems and processes that allow me to open the business, see to its functional operations, and hand off tasks and duties to others. From that point forward, I become the leader who oversees a project rather than a worker who actually does the work.

My power team is the power behind my skill as an entrepreneur. I am a team builder, and with every business I open I will evaluate and determine what team members I need to create, build, and expand my enterprise. I know the success of any business will depend on having people in place who will do the tasks that need to be done on a daily basis.

Universal Law

I WILL BECOME A MASTER AT FOLLOWING THE MONEY!

Becoming a master at following the money means I know where the deals are that will bring me the highest level of profit, and I know how much people will spend and what they will spend it on both today and in the future. I choose my streams of income based upon the next trend and the next big boom. I know how to study the markets, and I know in advance when the markets and demand will peak.

I understand that business demand is cyclical. For this reason, I will master the ability to evaluate a business's potential profitability, what will work in today's market, and what may need to be modified in the future. For example, I understand that when we are experiencing an upheaval in real estate markets and foreclosure numbers are through the roof, a very strong demand will be created within the next two years for apartment rentals and mobile home parks I do not wait until this information hits the national news to act, however. Rather, I use my knowledge and experience about the housing and lending markets to anticipate opportunities and act accordingly. That way, I am in place and my potential for profit is at its peak.

I know how to research, analyze, and determine where the money will be spent long before the average business owner even suspects an opportunity will present itself.

I WILL CREATE MARKETING SYSTEMS FOR EVERY BUSINESS I BUILD

Marketing is the life-blood of every business; without customers or clients, the business cannot function. One of the most important systems of any business is its marketing plan. How I identify who my clients are, how I find them, how much I spend to get them, how often they will purchase, and what I do to educate them about my product or service will be a central part of every one of my marketing systems.

Marketing is about more than running an ad on the radio or printing a flyer—it is about branding, message, mission, and intent. Marketing is about educating the public so steady streams of people are consistently seeking me to fulfill their unmet needs.

I am a marketing machine, and I have a program in place that maps out a strategy and a plan that meets the needs of my businesses on a consistent basis. I always have a plan in place, and I always have a budget to execute that plan.

MY NOTES

 **Universal Law**

I WILL DEVELOP A DATABASE OF POTENTIAL BUYERS AND SELLERS OF MY PRODUCT OR SERVICE

Marketing is about finding the people who have a need for my product or service, and I will become a master at finding them. I understand that a business may have tremendous opportunity in terms of its product offering, but if it doesn't get the word out, no money will be made. Getting the word out begins with database development.

I will do whatever it takes to formulate and execute a plan that draws prospective clients into my database. That often begins with telling everyone I know about my business and asking them to tell everyone they know. Before long, word-of-mouth advertising has people asking me about my business. My marketing plan will specifically be designed to grow my database. I will have a power team in place to direct potential buyers in the next step towards a purchase.

My database will grow, and I will use that database on a consistent basis to provide information, keep people informed of new offerings and services, and invite them to buy. My database is a top priority, and if I build it right, the people will come!

 **Universal Law**

I WILL NEVER CONTRACT TO BUY
A PROPERTY UNLESS I ALREADY HAVE
IT SOLD, ASSIGNED, OR A TENANT
TO PUT IN IT

Most real estate investors go out and find a house, close on the property, and then place an ad in the paper hoping to find a tenant who will rent or lease it to. Big mistake! When investors leave themselves open to vacancies, they are leaving themselves open to risk.

Before I contract to buy a house, I have already set my marketing plan in motion and begun the process of interviewing people who are looking for opportunities to either buy or lease in that area. I have mastered the steps of following the money, so I know what neighborhoods are the most desirable. As an entrepreneur I have mastered the steps to finding tenants, tenant buyers, and quick turn buyers. They are already in my database. Now, we can agree on where they can afford to live, and I can match my search for a property with their unmet needs. What does that create? Win/win solutions for everyone, and low risk for me!

I WILL DEVELOP A DATABASE OF REAL ESTATE INVESTORS

One of the ways I will begin building large amounts of earned income will involve finding properties that I can quick turn to others. This will allow me to begin a stream of earned income that is often referred to as wholesaling—the contracting of property and the selling of those contracts.

In order to make this business work successfully from the beginning, I must find investors who are interested in buying certain types of properties and then find the perfect property for them. I must have strong skills in negotiation, contract strategies, and creating win/win solutions. Since this is an early stream of income for me, I know how important it is to have contract clauses built into the purchase contract to protect both me and my contract buyer. As I build my database of investors, I will obtain information on how quickly they want to close, what type of property they are looking for, and where they want to invest.

I will always remember that my database will move me toward wealth safely and quickly. Building it, then, will be a top priority as I begin my wholesale stream of income.

MY NOTES

 **Universal Law**

I WILL ALWAYS FIND THE MONEY FIRST!

I know there is more money out there than I will ever need. However, I also know it takes time, effort, and expertise to master the skills of moving the money from a lender's account to mine. I am committed to mastering those skills, and I will be consistent in my approach to accessing funds.

As I begin contracting and purchasing businesses or buildings, I will always remember that the worst time to look for funding is when I am under time constraints and desperately in need of it. For that reason, I will always find the money before I need it.

I will become a money-finding machine. I will live by the law of finding the money early, that way, when I find an opportunity, the money will already be there. I am always, in all ways, sourcing capital for my investments.

MY NOTES

 **Universal Law**

I WILL BE THE CREATOR OF MY FUTURE

The average American wakes up each morning and goes to work living by someone else's rules, for their entire lives, they have been programmed that this is what is right and normal. As a leader and as an entrepreneur, I understand and embrace the knowledge that I have the ability to make the rules I live my life by.

Life is not luck; it is what I decide to create. I have choices about how I decide to live and how I create wealth. I write the rules of my life. It doesn't matter what it takes for me to succeed, because my circumstances don't drive my passion or my actions. My dream of leaving a legacy behind and my commitment to future generations drives my choices. My choice and my declaration is to live my life with the knowledge and acceptance of the fact that I am the creator of my future.

As the creator of my future and my destiny, I commit to mastering The Laws of Being an Entrepreneur. I know that as I put them into practice on a daily basis, I will have the tools to create a legacy and fulfill my burning desire of financial freedom and abundance.

Start Creating
Your Generational Legacy Today!

Get a free audio recording and complimentary access to wealth and legacy resources to help you create your generational legacy when you join my exclusive Entrepreneur Zone.

Visit: MentorFactor.com
Select 'Entrepreneur Zone'
and Become a Member!

In addition to the free audio recording you receive just for joining, my Entrepreneur Zone will give you immediate access to:

- Wealth and Legacy Videos
- Motivational Audios
- E-book Downloads
- Resources and Tools
- Weekly Entrepreneurship Ideas

Stay Empowered… Stay Encouraged… Take Action Today!

Visit www.MentorFactor.com and Become a Member of My Entrepreneur Zone—I'll be with You Every Step of the Way.

—Greg

**Together We Can Set in Motion,
a Change That Will Change the World**

Gregory S. Downing has dedicated his life to teaching his students that every family can truly control its financial future and create a generational legacy with profound, yet straightforward advice and guidance. As a highly respected and nationally recognized author, speaker, , family expert, and organizational consultant, his advice has been sought and put into practice by thousands of people from all walks of life. With over twenty years of experience in management, leadership, training, and business ownership, he has proven that his principles of legacy parenting, business promotion, entrepreneurship, and real estate investing work and create bonds of relationship that go beyond the ordinary.

Prior to his writing and public speaking career, he served for twelve years as the general manager of four Chevrolet and Dodge Chrysler dealerships, managing over 130 employees and increasing production and sales without sacrificing quality and customer service. It was during his tenure in this position that he became increasingly aware that his gift and talents were in motivating and leading others to achieve their goals and dreams. For that reason, he made the transition to motivational and investment training so he could touch more lives and influence others to build wealth and prosperity for themselves and for their families. When he saw first-hand how much families needed workable solutions to economic problems, he began expanding his focus to teach others how to build wealth within their family and create legacies that would last for generations to come.

Greg's vision is for goal-focused families across America to create generational legacies for their children. A business man by nature, education, and acquired knowledge, Downing is thoroughly prepared to lead your family to prosperity and financial independence as he shares his vision, determination, and strong business acumen.